W9-AUI-450

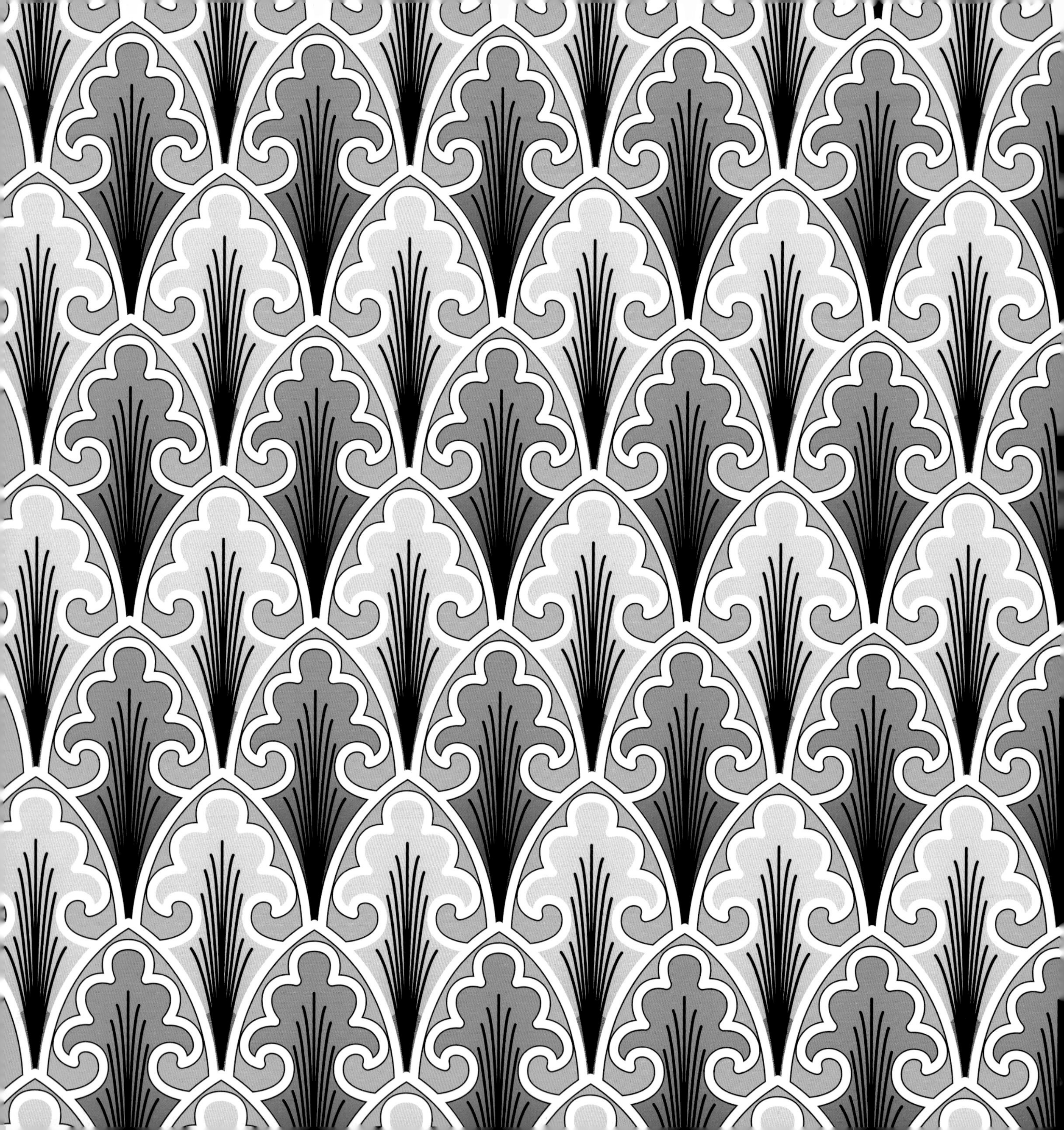

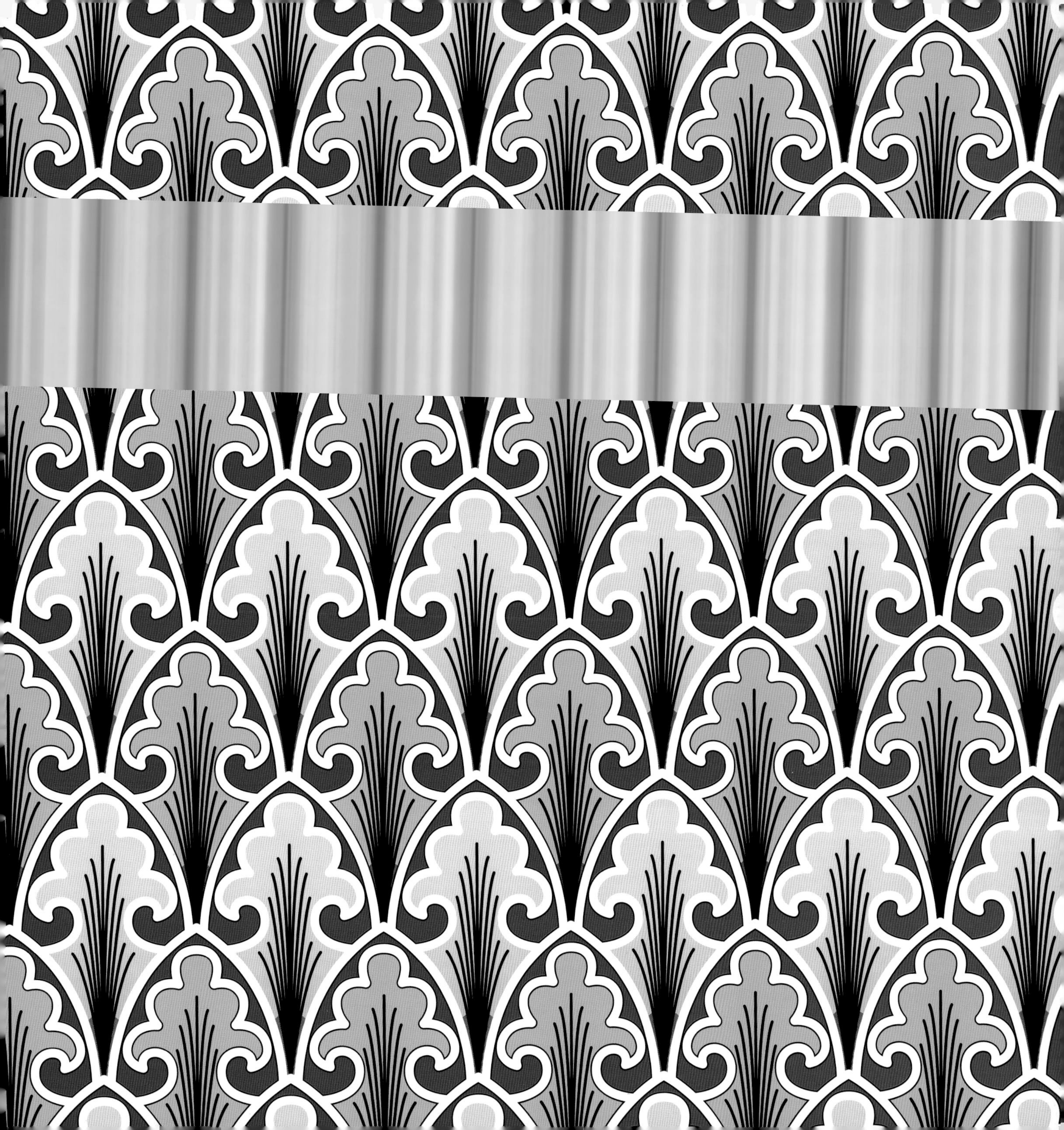

COLOPHON

The Pepin Press | Agile Rabbit Editions
P.O. Box 10349
1001 EH Amsterdam, The Netherlands

Translations: LocTeam, Barcelona
(Spanish, Italian, French, and German),
Michie Yamakawa, Tokyo (Japanese),
and TheBigWord, Leeds (Chinese)

ISBN 978 90 5768 092 2

10 9 8 7 6 5 4 3 2
2012 11 10 09 08

Manufactured in Singapore

CONTENTS

Free CD-Rom in the inside back cover

THE PEPIN PRESS / AGILE RABBIT EDITIONS

GRAPHIC THEMES
Fancy Alphabets
Mini Icons
Signs & Symbols
1000 Decorated Initials
Graphic Frames
Graphic Ornaments
Compendium of Illustrations
Teknological
Geometric Patterns
Classical Border Designs

PICTURE COLLECTIONS
Skeletons
Images of the Human Body
Bacteria And Other Micro Organisms
Erotic Images & Alphabets
5000 Animals (4 CDs)
Occult Images
Menu Designs

STYLES (HISTORICAL)
Early Christian Patterns
Byzanthine Patterns
Mediæval Patterns (Romanesque)
Gothic Patterns
Renaissance Patterns
Baroque Patterns
Rococo Patterns
Patterns of the 19th Century
Art Nouveau Designs
Jugendstil
Art Deco Designs
Fancy Designs 1920
Patterns of the 1930s

STYLES (CULTURAL)
Elements of Chinese & Japanese Design
Chinese Patterns
Japanese Patterns
Indian Textile Prints
Ancient Mexican Designs
Turkish Designs
Persian Designs
Islamic Designs
Arabian Geometric Patterns
Traditional Dutch Tile Designs
Tile Designs from Portugal
Barcelona Tile Designs

TEXTILE PATTERNS
Batik Patterns
Weaving Patterns
Lace
Embroidery
Ikat Patterns
Indian Textiles
Flower Power
European Folk Patterns
Kimono Patterns

FOLDING & PACKAGING
How To Fold
Folding Patterns for Display & Publicity
Structural Package Designs
Mail It!
Special Packaging

WEB DESIGN
Web Design Index 5
Web Design Index 6
Web Design by Content
Web Design by Content.02

PHOTOGRAPHS
Fruit
Vegetables
Female Body Parts
Male Body Parts
Body Parts in Black & White
Images of the Universe
Non Facturé – Rejected Photographs
Flowers

MISCELLANEOUS
Floral Patterns
Astrology Pictures
Historical & Curious Maps
Mythology Pictures
Wallpaper Designs
Watercolour Patterns

PEPIN PRESS FASHION BOOKS
Bags
Spectacles & Sunglasses
Figure Drawing for Fashion Design
Wrap-Around Fashion Design
Fashion Design 1800–1940
Art Deco Fashion
Traditional Henna Design
Fashion Accessories
Hairstyles of the World

More titles in preparation. In addition to the Agile Rabbit series of book +CD-ROM sets, The Pepin Press publishes a wide range of books on art, design, architecture, applied art, and popular culture.

Please visit www.pepinpress.com for more information.

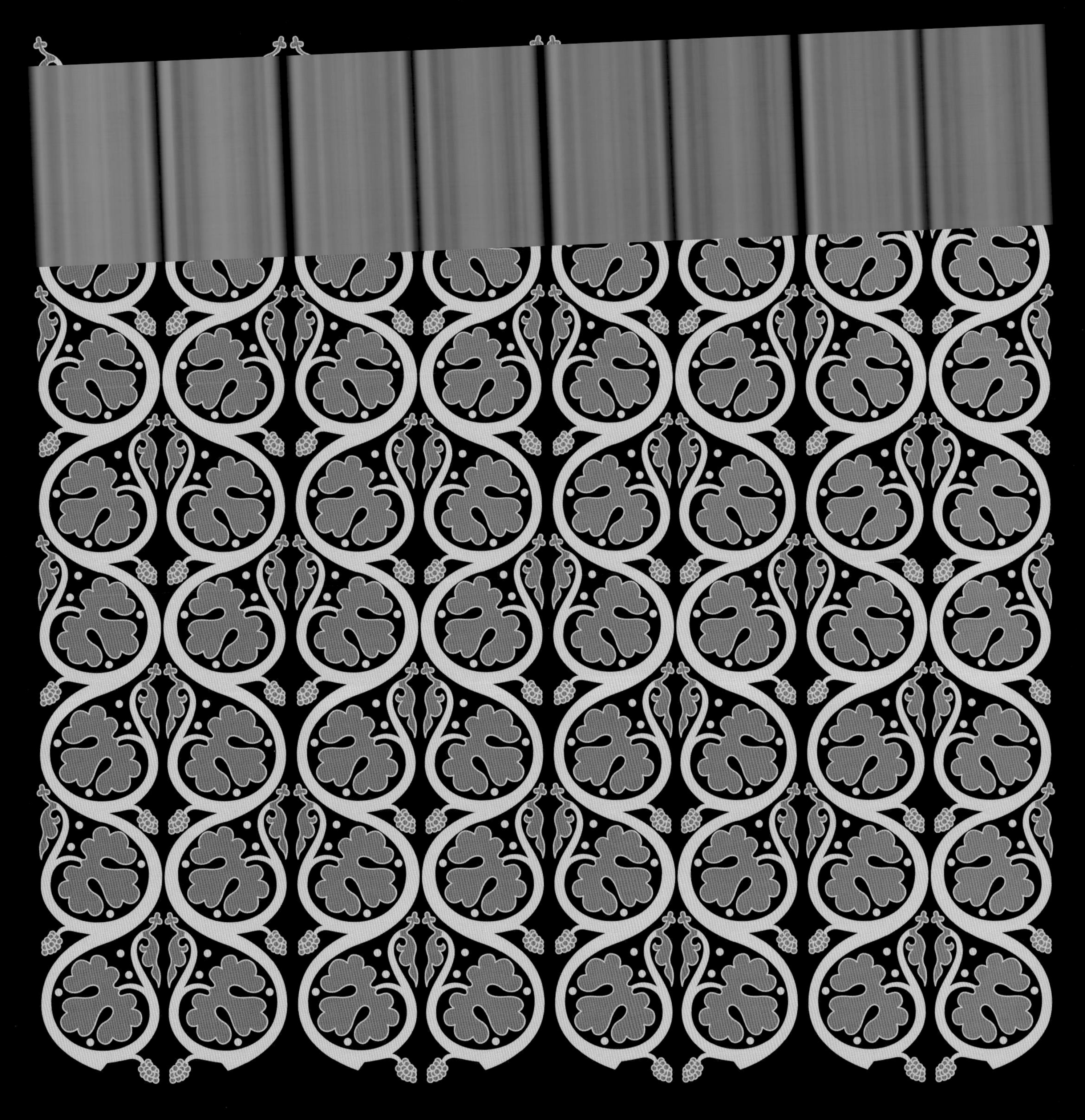

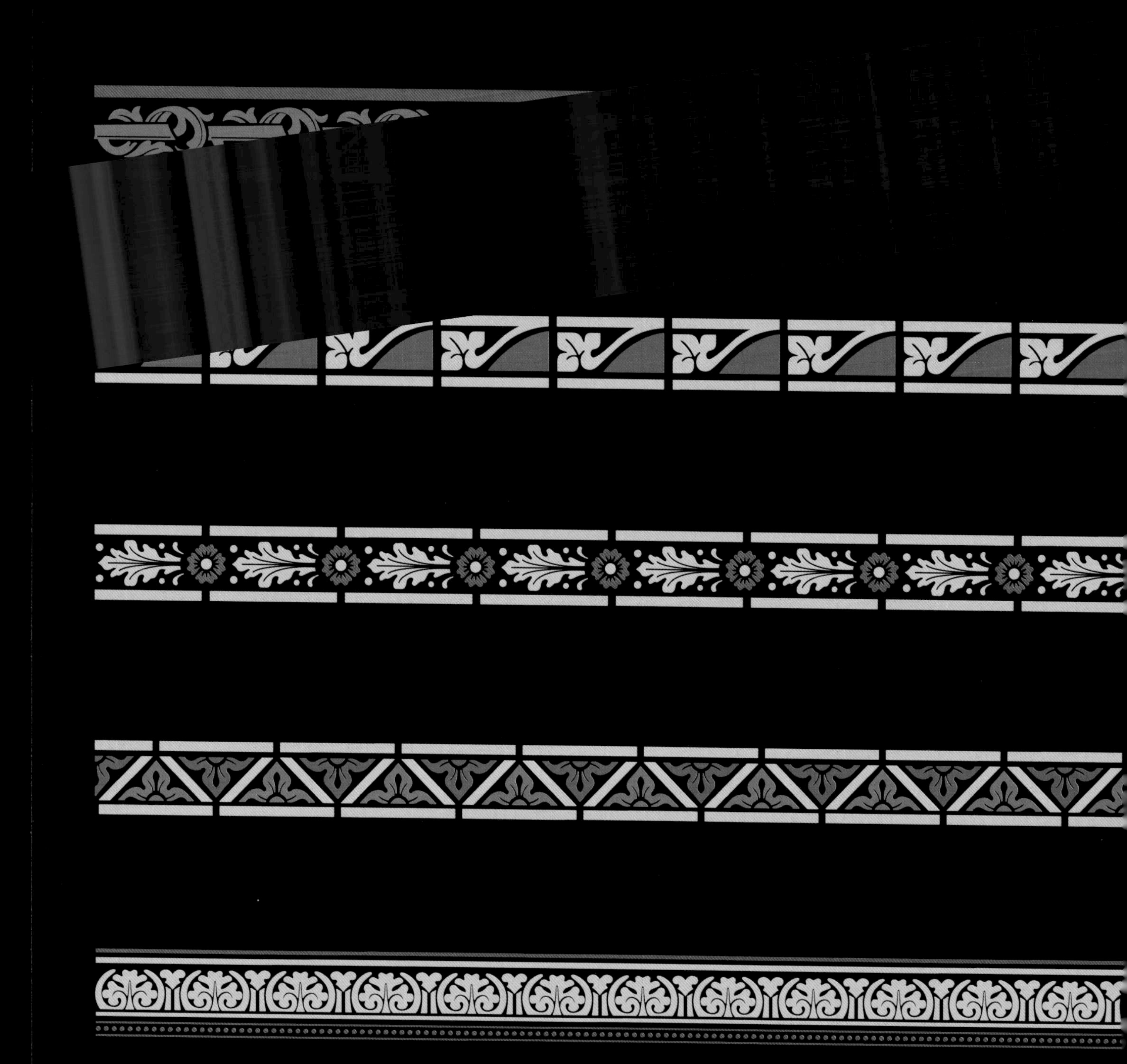

THE PEPIN PRESS / AGILE RABBIT EDITIONS

The Pepin Press / Agile Rabbit Editions book and CD-ROM sets offer a wealth of visual information and ready-to-use material for creative people. We publish various series as part of this line: graphic themes and pictures, photographs, packaging, web design, textile patterns, styles as defined by culture and the historical epochs that have generated a distinctive ornamental style. A list of available and forthcoming titles can be found at the beginning of this book. Many more volumes are being readied for publication, so we suggest you check our website from time to time for new additions.

EUROPEAN DESIGN 200 – 1900 AD

The present volume is part of a series that covers the decorative styles prevalent in Europe since the beginning of the Western calendar. Because of the practical nature of this series, we tend to focus on two-dimensional design, often culled from fabrics, wall coverings and printed paper, but also from patterns used to decorate flat surfaces in other forms of applied arts, such as furniture and metalwork. The original drawings are meticulously restored and often vectorised.

This series begins with the archaic styles of the Early Christian period (2nd to 7th centuries AD), the Byzantine (5th to 15th centuries) and the subsequent Mediæval epochs, including the Romanesque (10th to mid-12th centuries) and Late Gothic (13th and 14th centuries).
Although sometimes looked down upon because they were believed not to match the sophistication of the arts from ancient Rome, Mediæval pattern design and ornamentation, with their austere use of colour and rudimentary forms, can be of stunning harmony and beauty.

A revival of interest in the classical arts of Ancient Greece and Rome came with the Renaissance in the 15th and 16th centuries. Although the sculpture and architectural ornamentation during the Renaissance tended to be complex, two-dimensional patterns were often more subdued. The repetitive designs of the Renaissance can sometimes be confused with those of the Gothic period.

The predominant style of the 17th and first half of the 18th centuries was the Baroque. The applied arts from this period are characterised by the use of bold, sometimes overstated forms, including exaggerated curves and curlicues. While the floral compositions from the Baroque were often overpowering, the Rococo – the predominantly French style from the mid-18th century – displayed flowers in a more elegant fashion. During this period, the use of exquisite bouquets as a decorative detail became very popular.
The latter part of the 18th century showed the rise of two apparently opposing styles: the rather strict Neoclassicism and the joyful Romanticism. Both styles thrived until the mid-19th century.

In general, 19th century design was not particularly innovative, though it was highly eclectic. The great styles from the past were revived and often combined with stylistic discoveries from

Europe's numerou…

…nspiration. All the illustra-
…format on the enclosed free CD-ROM and are ready to use for
professional quality printed media and web page design.
The pictures can also be used to produce postcards, either on paper or digitally, or to decorate your letters, flyers, etc. They can be imported directly from the CD into most design, image-manipulation, illustration, word-processing and e-mail programs. Some programs will allow you to access the images directly; in others, you will first have to create a document, and then import the images. Please consult your software manual for instructions.
The names of the files on the CD-ROM correspond with the page numbers in this book. The CD-ROM comes free with this book, but is not for sale separately. The publishers do not accept any responsibility should the CD not be compatible with your system.
For non-professional applications, single images can be used free of charge. The images cannot be used for any type of commercial or otherwise professional application – including all types of printed or digital publications – without prior permission from The Pepin Press / Agile Rabbit Editions.

The files on Pepin Press/Agile Rabbit CD-ROMs are high quality and sufficiently large for most applications. However, larger and/or vectorised files are available for most images and can be ordered from The Pepin Press / Agile Rabbit Editions.

For inquiries about permissions and fees, please contact:
mail@pepinpress.com
Fax +31 20 4201152

THE PEPIN PRESS / AGILE RABBIT EDITIONS

Die aus Buch und CD-ROM bestehenden Sets von The Pepin Press / Agile Rabbit Editions bieten eine Fülle an visuellen Informationen und sofort verwendbarem Material für kreative Menschen. Im Rahmen dieser Reihe veröffentlichen wir verschiedene Serien: grafische Themen und Bilder, Fotos, Aufmachungen, Webdesigns, Stoffmuster sowie von Kulturströmungen und geschichtlichen Epochen geprägte Stilrichtungen, die eine eigene dekorative Stilrichtung hervorgebracht haben. Eine Liste der verfügbaren und kommenden Titel finden Sie am Anfang dieses Buchs. Viele weitere Bände befinden sich gerade in Vorbereitung – besuchen Sie daher regelmäßig unsere Website, um sich über Neuerscheinungen zu informieren.

EUROPÄISCHES DESIGN 200 - 1900 n. Chr.

Der vorliegende Band ist Teil einer Serie, die die in Europa seit Beginn des westlichen Kalenders vorherrschenden dekorative Stilrichtungen umfasst. Aufgrund der praktischen Ausrichtung der Serie konzentrieren wir uns vorrangig auf zweidimensionale Designs, die oft auf Stoffmuster, Wandtapeten und bedrucktes Papier zurückgehen, aber ebenso auf Mustern basieren, die zur Dekoration von glatten Oberflächen in anderen Bereichen der angewandten Kunst, wie beispielsweise Möbel und Metallarbeit, verwendet wurden. Die ursprünglichen Zeichnungen wurden minuziös rekonstruiert und in vielen Fällen vektorisiert.

Die vorliegende Serie beginnt mit den altertümlichen Stilrichtungen der frühchristlichen Periode (2. bis 7. Jahrhundert n. Chr.), der byzantinischen Epoche (5. bis 15. Jahrhundert) und den darauffolgenden Epochen des Mittelalters, einschließlich der Romanik (10. bis Mitte des 12. Jahrhundert) und der Spätgotik (13. und 14. Jahrhundert).
Obwohl mittelalterliche Muster manchmal geringgeschätzt wurden, da man meinte, dass diesen die Raffinesse der Künste des antiken Roms fehlten, überzeugen mittelalterliche Designs und Ornamente mit ihrer strengen Farbgebung und ihren rudimentären Formen durch eine erstaunliche Harmonie und Schönheit.

Mit der Renaissance des 15. und 16. Jahrhunderts kam es zu einem erneuten Aufleben des Interesses für die klassische Kunst des antiken Griechenlands und Roms. Während die Skulpturen und architektonischen Ornamente in der Renaissance eher komplexe Designs aufwiesen, waren die zweidimensionalen Muster oft eher dezent. Die sich wiederholenden Muster der Renaissance können leicht mit jenen der Gotik verwechselt werden.

Das 17. Jahrhundert stand ebenso wie die erste Hälfte des 18. Jahrhunderts ganz im Zeichen des Barock. Die angewandten Künste dieser Periode sind von kühnen, manchmal übertriebenen Formen, sowie ausschweifenden Kurven und Schnörkeln geprägt. Während die floralen Kompositionen des Barock oft überladen wirkten, wurden im Rokoko – dem vorwiegend französischen Stil aus der Mitte des 18. Jahrhunderts – Blumen in einer eleganteren Art und Weise zum Ausdruck gebracht. In dieser Periode erfreute sich die Verwendung exquisiter Blumensträuße als dekoratives Detail immer größerer Beliebtheit.

verbunden. Doch am Ende des 19. Jahrhunderts entstand mit dem Art Nouveau eine wahrlich neue Stilrichtung, die trotz ihrer Vielseitigkeit einen radikalen Bruch mit der klassischen Ornamentierung darstellte.

BUCH UND CD-ROM

Dieses Buch enthält Bilder, die als Ausgangsmaterial für graphische Zwecke oder als Anregung genutzt werden können. Alle Abbildungen sind in hoher Auflösung auf der beiliegenden Gratis-CD-ROM gespeichert und lassen sich direkt zum Drucken in professioneller Qualität oder zur Gestaltung von Websites einsetzen.
Sie können sie auch als Motive für Postkarten auf Karton oder in digitaler Form, oder als Ausschmückung für Ihre Briefe, Flyer etc. verwenden. Die Bilder lassen sich direkt in die meisten Zeichen-, Bildbearbeitungs-, Illustrations-, Textverarbeitungs- und E-Mail-Programme laden, ohne dass zusätzliche Programme installiert werden müssen. In einigen Programmen können die Dokumente direkt geladen werden, in anderen müssen Sie zuerst ein Dokument anlegen und können dann die Datei importieren. Genauere Hinweise dazu finden Sie im Handbuch zu Ihrer Software.
Die Namen der Bilddateien auf der CD-ROM entsprechen den Seitenzahlen dieses Buchs. Die CD-ROM wird kostenlos mit dem Buch geliefert und ist nicht separat verkäuflich. Der Verlag haftet nicht für Inkompatibilität der CD-ROM mit Ihrem System.
Für nicht professionelle Anwendungen können einzelne Bilder kostenfrei genutzt werden. Die Bilder dürfen ohne vorherige Genehmigung von The Pepin Press / Agile Rabbit Editions nicht für kommerzielle oder sonstige professionelle Anwendungen einschließlich aller Arten von gedruckten oder digitalen Medien eingesetzt werden.

Die Dateien auf den CD-ROMs sind in Bezug auf Qualität und Größe für die meisten Anwendungsbereiche geeignet. Zusätzlich können jedoch größere Dateien oder Vektorgrafiken der meisten Bilder bei The Pepin Press/Agile Rabbit Editions bestellt werden.

Für Fragen zu Genehmigungen und Preisen wenden Sie sich bitte an:
mail@pepinpress.com
Fax +31 20 4201152

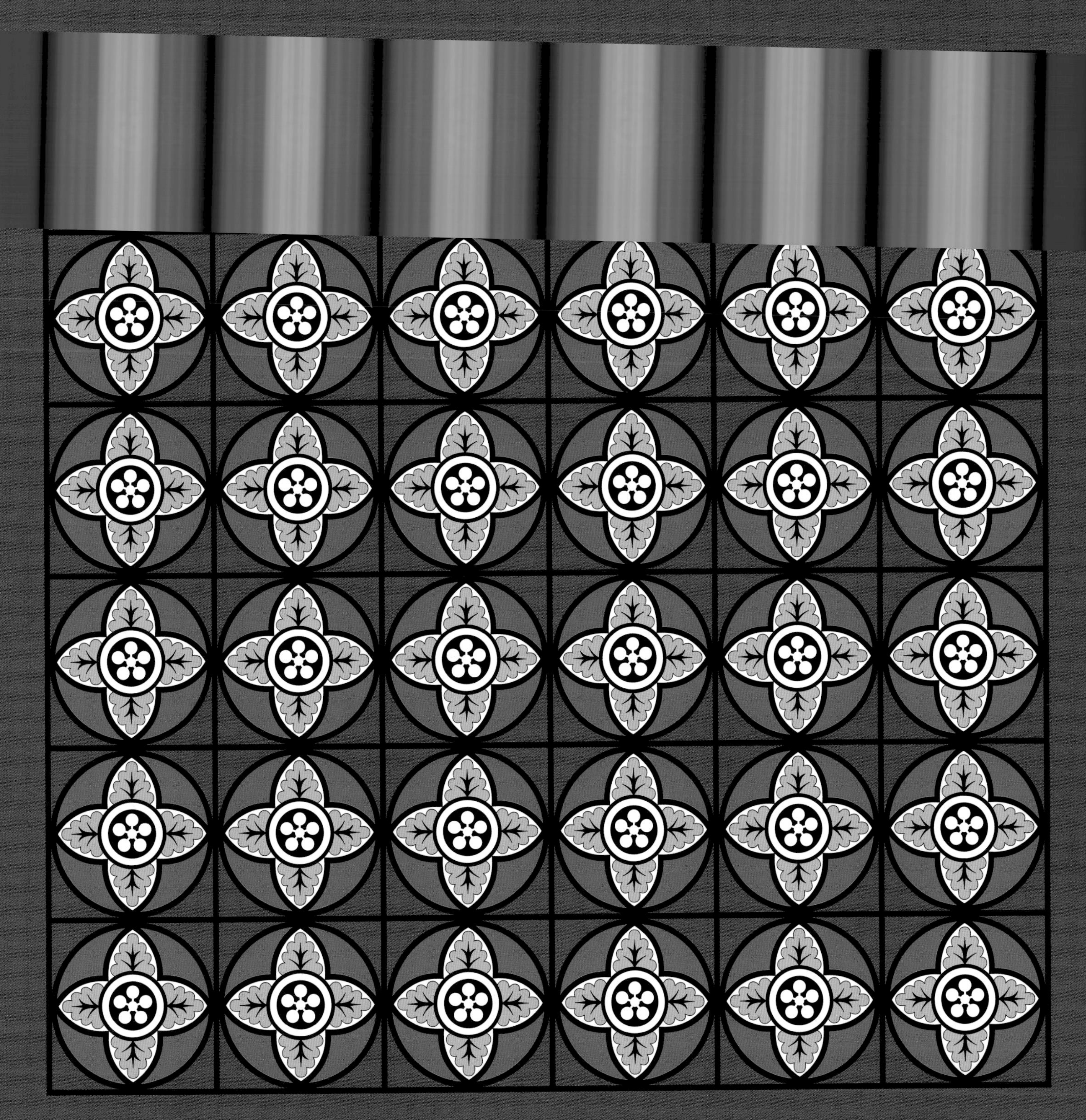

THE PEPIN PRESS / AGILE RABBIT EDITIONS

Les coffrets Livre + CD-ROM des éditions Pepin Press / Agile Rabbit proposent aux esprits créatifs une mine d'informations visuelles et de documents prêts à l'emploi. Dans le cadre de cette collection, nous publions plusieurs séries : thèmes et images graphiques, photographies, packaging, création de sites web, motifs textiles, styles tels qu'ils sont définis par chaque cultureet époques de l'histoire ayant engendré un style ornemental caractéristique. Vous trouverez une liste des titres disponibles et à venir au début de cet ouvrage. De nombreux autres volumes étant en cours de préparation, nous vous suggérons de consulter notre site web de temps à autre pour prendre connaissance des nouveautés.

ORNEMENTATION EUROPÉENNE DU 3ÈME AU 20ÈME SIÉCLE APRÉS J-C

Le présent volume fait partie d'une série traitant des styles décoratifs répandus en Europe depuis le début du calendrier occidental. Étant donné le caractère pratique de cette série, nous avons essayé de nous concentrer sur une ornementation bidimensionnelle, souvent sélectionnée parmi des tissus, des revêtements muraux et des papiers imprimés mais également parmi des motifs utilisés pour décorer des surfaces planes dans d'autres formes d'arts appliqués, comme celles du mobilier et de la ferronnerie. Les dessins originaux sont reproduits méticuleusement et souvent vectorisés.

Cette série commence par les styles archaïques du début de la période chrétienne (du 2ème au 7ème siècles après J-C), le byzantin (5ème au 15ème siècles) et les époques médiévales postérieures, y compris la période romane (du 10ème siècle jusqu'à la moitié du 12ème siècle) et la fin du gothique (13ème et 14ème siècles).
Bien que parfois méprisés car loin d'égaler la sophistication des arts de la Rome antique selon certains, le dessin et l'ornementation du style médiéval peuvent être d'une beauté et d'une harmonie remarquables, avec leur utilisation austère de la couleur et leurs formes rudimentaires.

Un regain d'intérêt pour les arts classiques de la Grèce et la Rome antiques est apparu avec la Renaissance aux 15ème et 16ème siècles. Si pendant la Renaissance la sculpture et l'ornementation architecturale avaient tendance à être complexes, les motifs bidimensionnels étaient souvent plus atténués. On peut parfois confondre les motifs répétitifs de la Renaissance avec ceux de la période gothique.

Le style prédominant du 17ème siècle et de la première moitié du 18ème siècle était le baroque. Les arts appliqués de cette période sont caractérisés par l'usage de formes hardies, parfois exagérées, et même de courbes et fioritures excessives. Tandis que les compositions florales du baroque étaient souvent oppressantes, le rococo - style principalement français du milieu du 18ème siècle - disposait les fleurs de manière plus élégante. Pendant cette période, l'usage de bouquets raffinés comme détail décoratif était très en vogue.

La dernière partie du 18ème siècle

décoration classique.

LIVRE ET CD-ROM

Cet ouvrage renferme des illustrations destinées à servir d'inspiration ou de ressources graphiques. Toutes les images sont stockées en format haute définition sur le CD-ROM et permettent la réalisation d'impressions de qualité professionnelle et la création de pages web. Elles permettent également de créer des cartes postales, aussi bien sur papier que virtuelles, ou d'agrémenter vos courriers, prospectus et autres.
Vous pouvez les importer directement à partir du CD dans la plupart des applications de création, manipulation graphique, illustration, traitement de texte et messagerie. Certaines applications permettent d'accéder directement aux images, tandis qu'avec d'autres, vous devrez d'abord créer un document, puis y importer les images. Veuillez consulter les instructions dans le manuel du logiciel concerné.

Sur le CD, les noms des fichiers correspondent aux numéros de pages du livre.
Le CD-ROM est fourni gratuitement avec le livre et ne peut être vendu séparément. L'éditeur décline toute responsabilité si ce CD n'est pas compatible avec votre ordinateur. Vous pouvez utiliser les images individuelles gratuitement avec des applications non-professionnelles. Il est interdit d'utiliser les images avec des applications de type professionnel ou commercial (y compris avec tout type de publication numérique ou imprimée) sans l'autorisation préalable des éditions Pepin Press / Agile Rabbit.

Les fichiers figurant sur les CD-ROM Pepin Press/Agile Rabbit sont de haute qualité et d'une taille acceptable pour la plupart des applications. Cependant, des fichiers plus volumineux et/ou vectorisés sont disponibles pour la plupart des images. Vous pouvez les commander auprès des Éditions The Pepin Press/Agile Rabbit.

Adresse électronique et numéro de télécopie à utiliser pour tout renseignement relatif aux autorisations et aux frais d'utilisation :
mail@pepinpress.com
Télécopie : +31 20 4201152

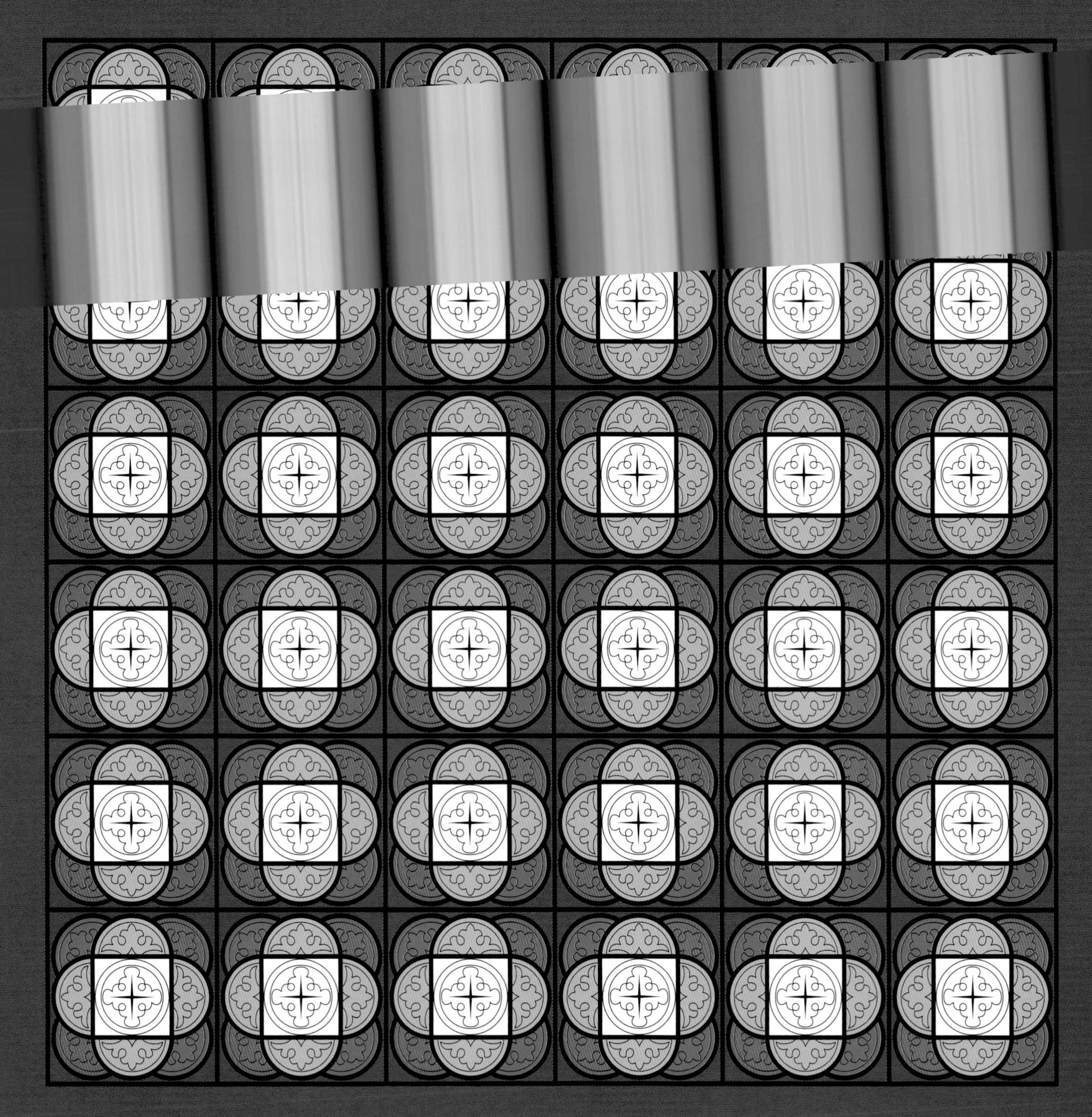

THE PEPIN PRESS / AGILE RABBIT EDITIONS

Los libros con CD-ROM incluido que nos propone The Pepin Press / Agile Rabbit Editions ponen a disposición de los creativos una amplísima información visual y material listo para ser utilizado. Dentro de la colección Agile Rabbit se publican diferentes series: motivos gráficos e ilustraciones, fotografías, embalaje, diseño de páginas web, motivos textiles, y estilos definidos por una determinada cultura y por las épocas históricas que han generado un estilo ornamental distintivo. Al principio de este libro encontrará una lista de los títulos disponibles y en preparación. Estamos trabajando en muchos más volúmenes, por lo que le aconsejamos que visite periódicamente nuestra página web para estar informado de todas las novedades.

DISEÑO EUROPEO 200 - 1900 AD

Este libro forma parte de una colección dedicada a los estilos decorativos que prevalecieron en Europa desde la instauración del calendario occidental. A causa del carácter práctico de la misma, nos hemos centrado en el diseño bidimensional, que en muchas ocasiones hemos extraído de tejidos, decoraciones de paredes y papel impreso, sin por ello desdeñar los patrones utilizados para decorar superficies planas en otras manifestaciones de las artes aplicadas, como los muebles o el trabajo en metal. Los dibujos originales han sido restaurados meticulosamente y, a menudo, vectorizados.

Esta colección se inicia con los estilos arcaicos de principios de la era cristiana (siglos II a VII a.C.), el periodo bizantino (siglos V a XV) y los distintos periodos medievales, incluyendo el románico (siglo x a mediados del XII) y el gótico tardío (siglos XIII y XIV).
A pesar de que en ocasiones han sido menospreciados por no estar a la altura de la sofisticación del arte de la antigua Roma, el diseño y la ornamentación medievales, con su austero uso del color y sus formas rudimentarias, pueden alcanzar niveles sorprendentes de armonía y belleza.

Durante el Renacimiento, que se extiende entre los siglos XV y XVI, asistimos a un renovado interés por las artes clásicas de Grecia y Roma. A pesar de que la ornamentación renacentista aplicada a la escultura y la arquitectura tendían a la complejidad, a menudo los patrones bidimensionales eran más comedidos. En ocasiones, los diseños repetitivos de este periodo pueden confundirse con los de estilo gótico.

El siglo XVII y la primera mitad del XVIII fueron los años del barroco. Las artes aplicadas de esta era se caracterizan por el uso de formas enérgicas y a menudo exageradas, en las que no podían faltar las curvas y filigranas sin medida. Mientras que las composiciones florales del barroco resultaban a menudo demasiado pomposas, el rococó, un estilo que se desarrolló predominantemente en Francia a partir de mediados del siglo XVIII, recreó las flores de un modo más elegante. Durante esta etapa, gozó de gran popularidad la utilización de ramos exquisitos como detalle decorativo.
Durante la segunda mitad de este siglo asistimos al auge de dos estilos aparentemente opuestos:

el estricto neoclasicismo y el

CD-ROM

En este libro podrá encontrar imágenes que le servirán como fuente de material gráfico o como inspiración para realizar sus propios diseños. Se adjunta un CD-ROM gratuito donde hallará todas las ilustraciones en un formato de alta resolución, con las que podrá conseguir una impresión de calidad profesional y diseñar páginas web.
Las imágenes pueden también emplearse para realizar postales, de papel o digitales, o para decorar cartas, folletos, etc. Se pueden importar desde el CD a la mayoría de programas de diseño, manipulación de imágenes, dibujo, tratamiento de textos y correo electrónico, sin necesidad de utilizar un programa de instalación. Algunos programas le permitirán acceder a las imágenes directamente; otros, sin embargo, requieren la creación previa de un documento para importar las imágenes. Consulte su manual de software en caso de duda.
Los nombres de los archivos del CD-ROM se corresponden con los números de página de este libro. El CD-ROM se ofrece de manera gratuita con este libro, pero está prohibida su venta por separado. Los editores no asumen ninguna responsabilidad en el caso de que el CD no sea compatible con su sistema.
Se autoriza el uso de estas imágenes de manera gratuita para aplicaciones no profesionales. No se podrán emplear en aplicaciones de tipo profesional o comercial (incluido cualquier tipo de publicación impresa o digital) sin la autorización previa de The Pepin Press / Agile Rabbit Editions.

Los archivos incluidos en los CD-ROM de Pepin Press/Agile Rabbit son de alta calidad y de tamaño suficiente para cualquier utilidad. No obstante, pueden solicitarse a The Pepin Press/Agile Rabbit Editions archivos de mayor tamaño o archivos vectorizados de prácticamente todas las imágenes.

Para más información acerca de autorizaciones y tarifas:

mail@pepinpress.com
Fax +31 20 4201152

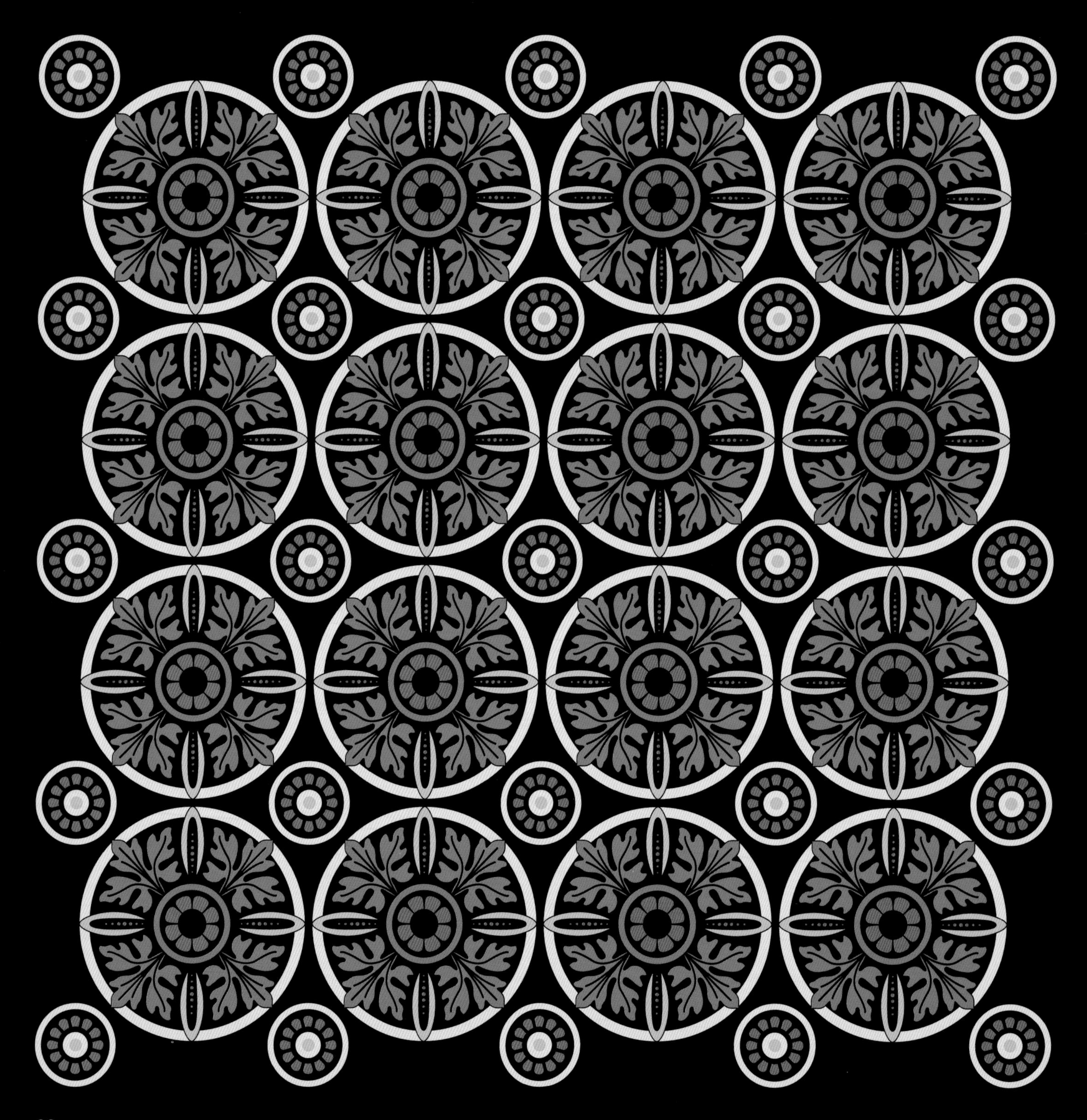

l libro della Pepin Press / Agile Rabbit Editions e l'accluso CD-ROM mettono a disposizione de creativi un ricco supporto visivo e materiale pronto per l'uso. La collana comprende diverse serie motivi grafici e illustrazioni, fotografie, packaging, web design, motivi per tessuti, stili secondo la definizione data dalla cultura e dalle epoche storiche che hanno prodotto uno stile ornamentale particolare. Nelle prime pagine del libro è riportato l'elenco delle opere già in catalogo e di quelle n via di pubblicazione. Sono molti gli altri testi in via di pubblicazione, quindi consigliamo di visitare periodicamente il nostro sito internet per essere informati sulle novità.

L DESIGN EUROPEO DAL 200 AL 1900

Questo volume fa parte di una serie dedicata agli stili decorativi che hanno dominato in Europa dall'avvento del calendario occidentale. Data la natura pratica di questa serie, tendiamo a richiamare l'attenzione sul design bidimensionale, spesso imitazione di tessuti, carte da parati e carta stampata, ma ricavato anche da motivi usati per decorare superfici piane in altre forme di art applicate, quali mobili e lavori su metallo. I disegni originali sono stati restaurati con molta cura e spesso vettorizzati.

La serie inizia dagli stili arcaici del primo periodo cristiano (II-VII secolo) e prosegue con il bizantino (V-XV secolo) e le successive epoche medievali, soffermandosi anche sul romanico (V-metà del XII secolo) e sul tardo gotico (XIII-XIV secolo).
Anche se a volte guardati dall'alto in basso perché non ritenuti in grado di reggere il confronto con la ricercatezza delle arti dell'antica Roma, il design e l'ornamento dei motivi medievali, con l'uso austero del colore e le forme rudimentali, possono raggiungere livelli stupefacenti di armonia e di bellezza.

Nel Rinascimento, nel XV-XVI secolo, si risvegliò l'interesse nei confronti delle arti classiche dell'antica Grecia e dell'antica Roma. Anche se la scultura e l'ornamento architettonico nel Rinascimento avevano la tendenza ad essere elaborati, i motivi bidimensionali furono spesso più smorzati. I motivi ripetitivi del Rinascimento si possono a volte confondere con quelli del periodo gotico.

Il barocco fu lo stile predominante del XVII secolo e della prima metà del XVIII. Le arti applicate di questo periodo sono caratterizzate dall'uso di forme ardite, a volte esagerate, con abbondanza di curve e volute. Se le composizioni floreali del barocco risultavano sovente troppo pompose il rococò, lo stile francese che si affermò intorno alla metà del XVIII secolo, è caratterizzato da un uso più elegante dell'elemento floreale. In questo periodo, l'utilizzo di raffinati bouquet come dettaglio decorativo diventò molto popolare.
L'ultima parte del XVIII secolo vide emergere due stili apparentemente opposti: il rigoroso neoclassicismo e il vivace romanticismo. Entrambi prosperarono fino alla metà del XIX secolo.

Questo libro contiene immagini che possono essere utilizzate come risorsa grafica o come fonte di ispirazione. La maggior parte delle illustrazioni sono contenute nel CD-ROM gratuito allegato, in formato ad alta risoluzione e pronte per essere utilizzate per pubblicazioni professionali e pagine web.
Possono essere inoltre usate per creare cartoline, su carta o digitali, o per abbellire lettere, opuscoli, ecc. Dal CD, le immagini possono essere importate direttamente nella maggior parte dei programmi di grafica, di ritocco, di illustrazione, di scrittura e di posta elettronica; non è richiesto alcun tipo di installazione. Alcuni programmi vi consentiranno di accedere alle immagini direttamente; in altri, invece, dovrete prima creare un documento e poi importare le immagini. Consultate il manuale del software per maggiori informazioni.
I nomi dei file del CD-ROM corrispondono ai numeri delle pagine del libro. Il CD-ROM è allegato gratuitamente al libro e non può essere venduto separatamente. L'editore non può essere ritenuto responsabile qualora il CD non fosse compatibile con il sistema posseduto.
Per le applicazioni non professionali, le singole immagini possono essere usate gratis. Per l'utilizzo delle immagini a scopo professionale o commerciale, comprese tutte le pubblicazioni digitali o stampate, è necessaria la relativa autorizzazione da parte della casa editrice The Pepin Press / Agile Rabbit Editions.

I file contenuti nei CD-ROM di Pepin Press/Agile Rabbit sono di alta qualità e di dimensioni sufficienti per le applicazioni più comuni. Tuttavia, per la maggior parte delle immagini, è possibile richiedere a The Pepin Press/Agile Rabbit Editions file più grandi e/o vettorializzati.

Per ulteriori informazioni rivolgetevi a:
mail@pepinpress.com
Fax +31 20 4201152

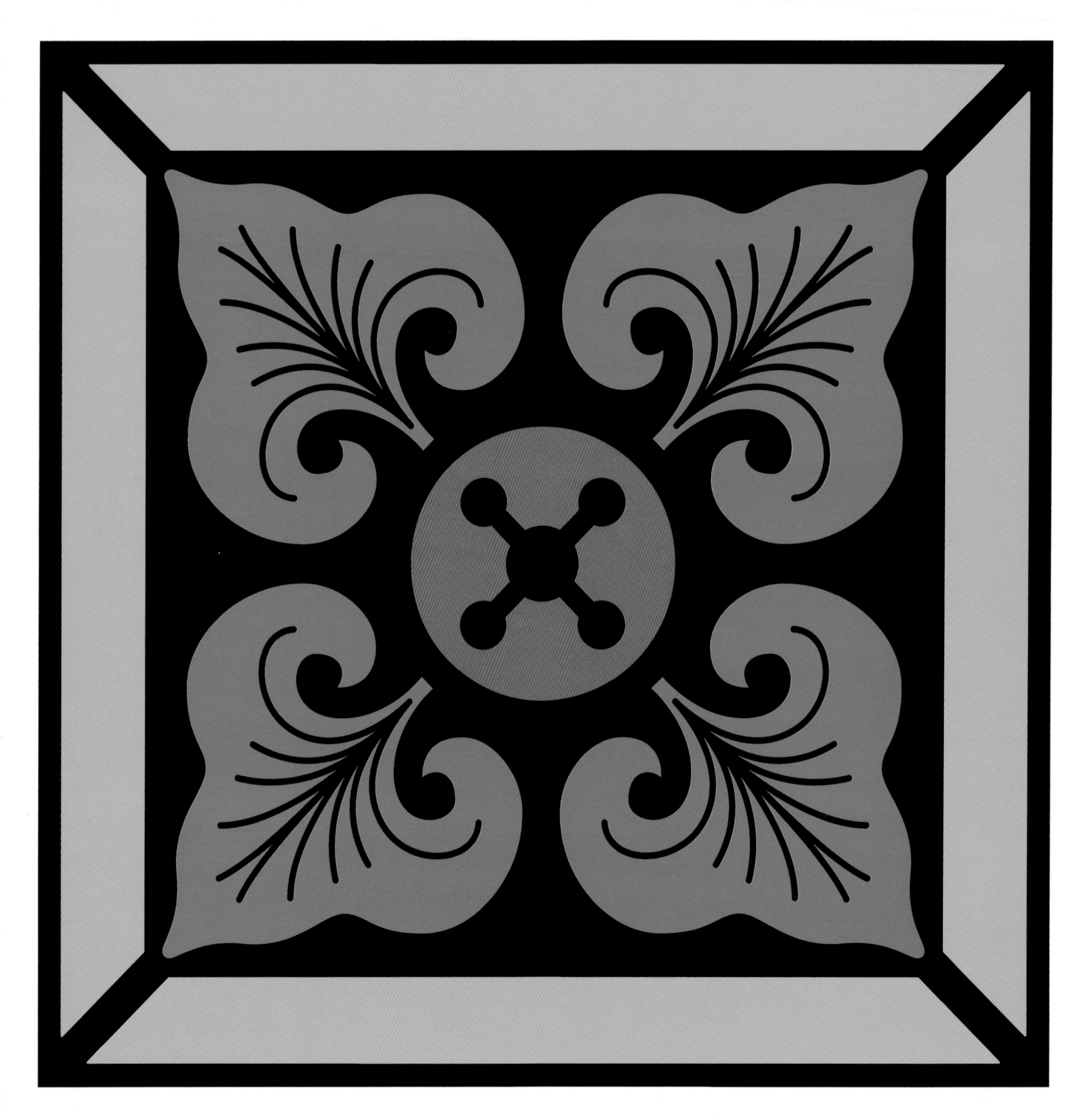

THE PEPIN PRESS / AGILE RABBIT EDITIONS

Os conjuntos de livro e CD-ROM da The Pepin Press / Agile Rabbit Editions proporcionam uma grande variedade de informações visuais e disponibilizam materiais prontos a utilizar por pessoas criativas. Nesta linha, publicamos várias séries: temas gráficos e imagens, fotografias, embalagens, design para a Web, padrões têxteis, estilos culturais e épocas históricas que produziram estilos ornamentais característicos. Nas primeiras páginas deste livro é apresentada uma lista de títulos já publicados e no prelo. Muitos mais estão em preparação, pelo que sugerimos que consulte regularmente o nosso sítio na Web para se inteirar das novidades.

DESIGN EUROPEU 200 - 1900

O presente volume faz parte de uma série que abrange os estilos decorativos prevalecentes na Europa desde o início do calendário ocidental. Dada a natureza prática desta série, privilegia-se o design bidimensional, muitas vezes copiado de tecidos, revestimentos de parede e papéis impressos, mas também de padrões usados para decorar superfícies planas noutras formas artísticas, como o mobiliário e a arte dos metais. Os desenhos originais foram meticulosamente restaurados e muitas vezes vectorizados.

Esta série começa com os estilos arcaicos do período Paleocristão (séc. II a VII), o Bizantino (séc. V a XV) e as épocas medievais seguintes, incluindo o Românico (séc. X a meados do séc. XII) e o Gótico tardio (séc. XIII e XIV).
Por vezes secundarizados por não serem considerados ao nível da sofisticação das artes da Roma antiga, os desenhos e ornamentos dos padrões medievais, com o seu uso austero da cor e formas rudimentares, podem encerrar em si uma extraordinária harmonia e beleza.

A Renascença, nos séculos XV e XVI, veio reavivar o interesse pelas artes clássicas da Grécia e da Roma antigas. Embora a escultura e a ornamentação arquitectónica na Renascença tendessem a ser complexas, os padrões bidimensionais eram bem mais contidos. Os desenhos repetitivos da Renascença podem, por vezes, confundir-se com os do período gótico.

O estilo dominante no século XVII e na primeira metade do século XVIII foi o Barroco. A produção artística desta época caracteriza-se pelo uso de formas ousadas, por vezes exageradas, incluindo curvas rebuscadas e ornatos. Enquanto que as composições florais do Barroco eram muitas vezes ostensivas, o Rococó, um estilo predominantemente francês de meados do século XVIII, retratava as flores de uma forma mais elegante. Durante este período, a utilização de arranjos florais requintados tornou-se muito frequente como pormenor decorativo.
Na segunda metade do século XVIII, assistiu-se à ascensão de dois estilos aparentemente antagónicos: o rigoroso Neoclassicismo e o jovial Romantismo. Ambos os estilos perduraram até meados do século XIX.
Em geral, o design no século XIX não foi particularmente inovador, mas era muito eclético. Recuperaram-se os grandes estilos do passado e foram muitas vezes combinados com descobertas

... podem ser utilizadas como recurso gráfico ou inspiração. Todas as ilustrações estão armazenadas no CD-ROM gratuito que acompanha o livro e estão prontas para serem utilizadas em materiais impressos de qualidade profissional e na concepção de páginas para a Web.
As imagens podem, também, ser utilizadas para criar postais, em papel ou digitais, ou para decorar cartas, panfletos, etc. Podem ser importadas directamente do CD para a maioria dos programas de desenho, manipulação de imagens, ilustração, processamento de texto e correio electrónico. Alguns programas permitem o acesso directo às imagens, ao passo que noutros é necessário criar primeiro um documento para, em seguida, importar para ele as imagens. Consulte o manual do software para obter instruções.
Os nomes dos ficheiros no CD-ROM correspondem aos números das páginas do livro. O CD-ROM é fornecido gratuitamente com este livro, mas não pode ser vendido separadamente. Os editores não assumem qualquer responsabilidade em caso de incompatibilidade do CD com o sistema operativo do utilizador.
A utilização de imagens individuais para aplicações não profissionais é gratuita. As imagens não podem ser utilizadas para nenhum tipo de aplicação comercial ou profissional, incluindo todo e qualquer tipo de publicação impressa ou digital, sem a prévia autorização da The Pepin Press/Agile Rabbit Editions.

Os ficheiros nos CD-ROMs da Pepin Press/Agile Rabbit são de alta qualidade e suficientemente grandes para a maioria das finalidades a que se destinam. Se necessário, é possível encomendar ficheiros maiores e/ou vectorizados da maioria das imagens à The Pepin Press/Agile Rabbit Editions.

Para obter esclarecimentos sobre autorizações e preços, contacte:
mail@pepinpress.com
Fax +31 20 4201152

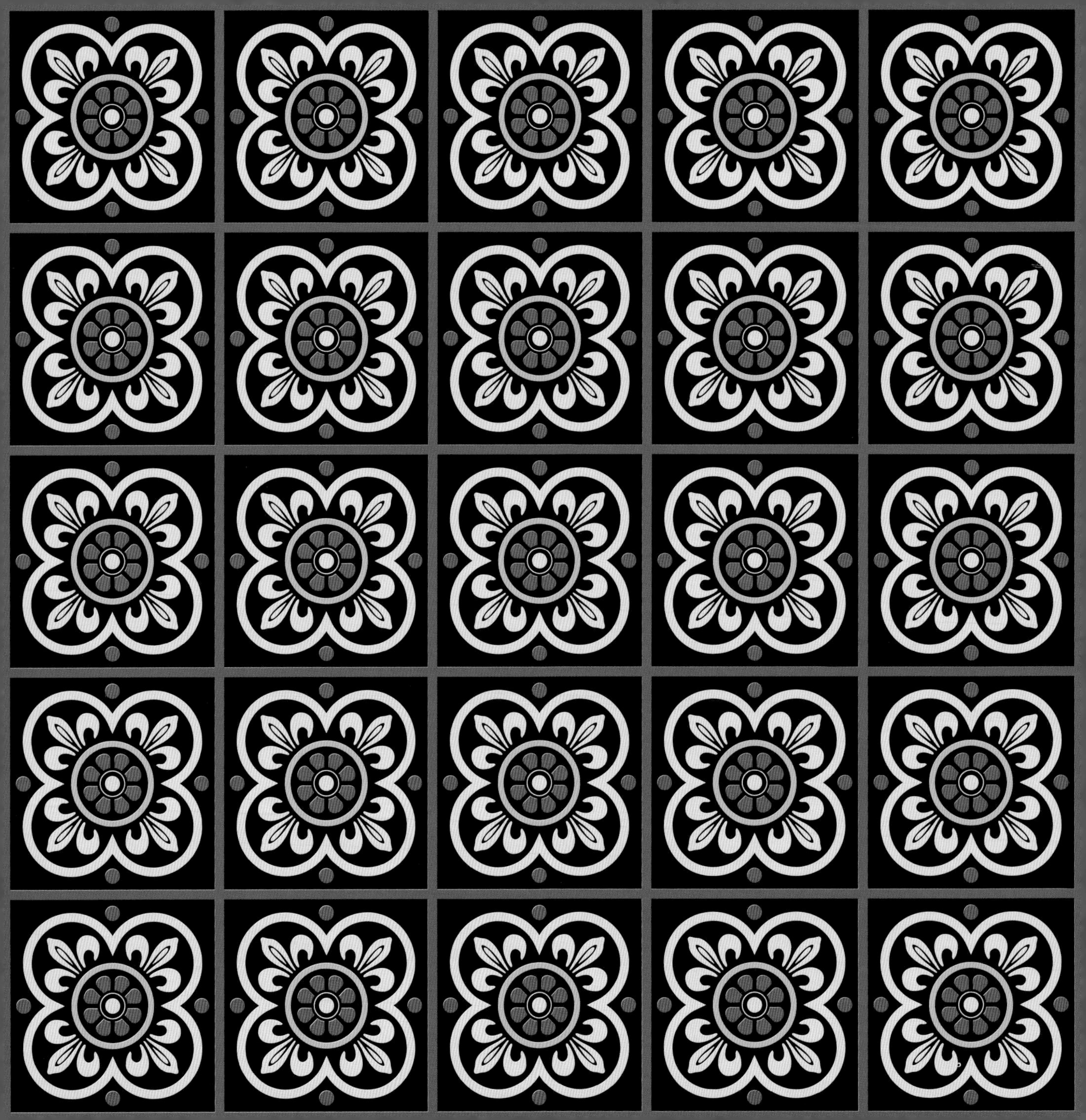

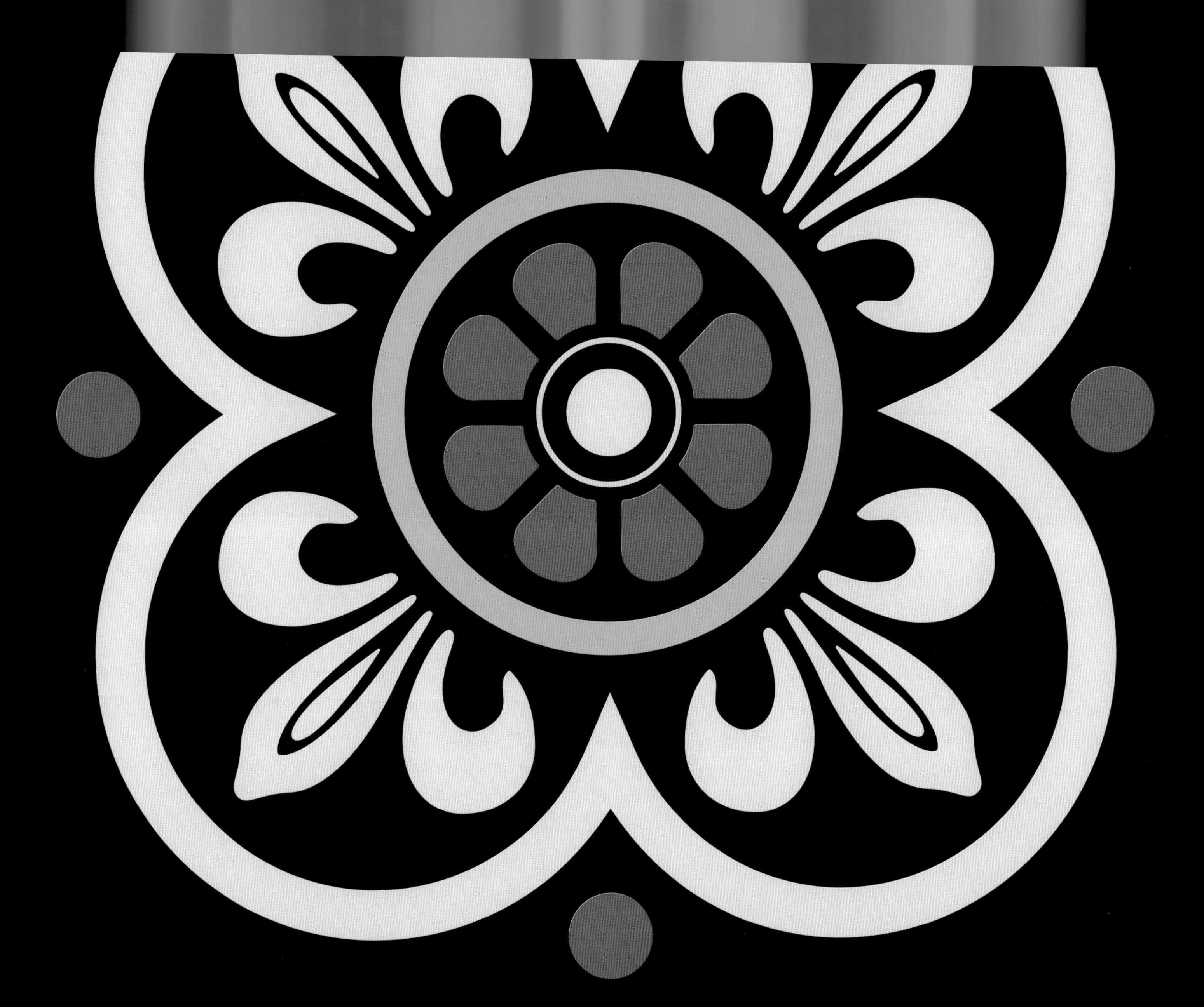

PEPIN出版社/AGILE RABBIT

Pepin出版社/Agile Rabbit图书和光盘向有创造力的人提供大量的视觉资料和便于使用的资料。我们出版各种系列：绘图主题和图片、照片、包装、网页设计以及不同文化和历史时代产生的不同装饰风格。本书的开头有已经和即将出版的各个标题。更多的丛书即将出版，因此我们建议您不时浏览我们的网站以得到这方面信息的更新。

欧洲设计 公元200年-1900年

本书是涵盖自西方日历开始后流行于欧洲的装饰风格的系列丛书之一。因为此丛书强调实用，因此我们的焦点集中在两维设计上，这些两维设计经常取材于纺织品、墙饰、包装纸以及以其它应用艺术形式如家具和金属制品用于装饰平坦表面的图案。图案的原貌得以精心的保存并常常向量化。

本套丛书首先论述古老的基督教早期风格（公元2-7世纪）、东罗马帝国时期（5-15世纪）风格以及后来的中世纪风格包括罗马风格（10世纪到12世纪中叶）以及后哥特式风格（13和14世纪）。
尽管中世纪图案设计和装饰因为被认为无法达到古罗马艺术的深度而有时受到轻视，但是其朴素的颜色和形式所产生的和谐和美也让人叹为观止。

随着15世纪和16世纪的文艺复兴，对古希腊和古罗马古典艺术的兴趣得到恢复。但文艺复兴时期雕塑和建筑装饰趋向复杂，两维图案常常被更多地削弱。文艺复兴时期的重复设计有时会同哥特时期的设计混淆。

17和18世纪上半叶的主要风格是巴洛克式。这一时期的应用艺术表现为使用突露的，有时甚至是夸张的形式，包括夸张的曲线和花体。巴洛克时期的花卉图案常常过于炫耀，而洛可可风格-主要是18世纪中期的法国风格-在展示花卉图案时则较优雅。使用优美的花束进行装饰在这一时期非常流行。
18世纪后半叶出现两种明显对立的风格：较严肃的新古典主义风格和轻松活泼的浪漫主义风格。这两种风格一直流行到19世纪中叶。

总体说来，19世纪的设计不是特别有新意，尽管其取材更加广泛。过去高超的风格在19世纪得到复兴并同欧洲大量的殖民地风格融合在一起。但是，在19世纪末出现了一种全新的风格-新艺术，这种风格尽管取材广泛，却从根本上脱离了古典装饰风格。

光盘上的文件名称同本书的页码对应。光盘随本书免费赠送，但不单独销售。如果光盘同您的系统不相容，出版商不承担任何责任。
对于非专业应用，单个图象免费使用。未经 Pepin Press/Agile Rabbit Editions 的事先允许，这些图片不得用于任何商业性或专业用途 – 包括所有类型的纸质或数字出版物。

Pepin Press/Agile Rabbit光盘上的文件质量可靠，对于大部分的应用都足够大。但是，大部分图象的更大和/或向量化文件可以向Pepin 出版社/Agile Rabbit订购。

有关许可权和费用咨询，请联系:
mail@pepinpress.com
传真 +31 20 4201152

ザ・ペピン・プレス/アジャイレ・ラビット・エディションズ

ザ・ペピン・プレス/アジャイレ・ラビット・エディションズの本とCD-ROMのセットは、豊富なビジュアル情報と、すぐにそのまま使用できる素材が入っています。当社は、グラフィックやイラスト、写真、パッケージ、ウェブ・デザイン、独自の装飾様式を生み出した文化と時代のテキスタイル・パターンなど、様々なシリーズを出版しています。既刊及び発行予定のタイトルのリストについては、この本の巻頭をごらんください。今後も、様々な物を出版する予定ですので、当社のウェブサイトを時々チェックしてください。

ヨーロッパのデザイン　西暦200年～1900年

本書は、西暦が始まってから、ヨーロッパで流行った装飾様式についてのシリーズの１巻です。このシリーズは、平面デザインにフォーカスを絞っています。掲載イメージは、織物や壁紙、印刷物のほか、家具や金属細工といった応用美術の平らな表面を飾った図案も含んでいます。オリジナルの描画が細部まで正確に修復されています。

このシリーズは、初期キリスト教時代（2世紀から７世紀）、ビザンチン時代（５世紀から15世紀）、ロマネスク時代（10世紀から12世紀半ば）と後期ゴシック時代（13世紀と14世紀）を含む中世の様式をカバーしています。中世の図案と装飾は、古代ローマの洗練された芸術に匹敵しないと信じられて、見過ごされがちですが、その限られた色使いと、未成熟なフォームにより、驚くべき調和と美を作り出しています。

古代ギリシア・ローマの古典芸術復興が起きたのは、15世紀と16世紀のルネッサンス時代です。この時代の彫刻と建築装飾は複雑で込み入っていますが、平面図案はもっとおとなしいスタイルでした。ルネッサンス時代の反復デザインは、ゴシック時代のそれとよく似ていたりもします。

17世紀と18世紀前半に流行したのはバロック様式です。この時代の応用美術の特徴は、誇張された曲線や渦巻きなど、大胆かつ大仰な形状です。バロック時代の花柄構図は、装飾過剰気味なのに対し、18世紀半ばから主にフランスで流行したロココ様式は、もっとエレガントに花をモチーフに用いました。この時代には、装飾のディテールとして、美しい花束を用いるのが大流行しました。

18世紀後半になると、ふたつの相反する様式が現れました。厳格な新古典主義と、楽しいロマン主義です。両方とも、19世紀半ばまで流行しました。

一般的に、19世紀のデザインは、非常に折衷的ではあったものの、とりたてて革新的というわけではありませんでした。過去の様式が復興し、ヨーロッパの数々の植民地で発見された様式と組み合わされました。しかし、19世紀終わりになると、アール・ヌーヴォーという新しい様式が登場しました。これは、折衷的ではありましたが、古典的な装飾とは劇的に異なる様式でした。

また、ハガキや手紙、チラシのイメージとしても使えます。[illegible]
できます。そうでない場合には、ファイルを作成し、イメージをインポートしてください。方法については、お手元のソフトウエアのマニュアルでご確認ください。

CD-ROMの各ファイル名は、この本のページ番号と同じです。CD-ROM は付録ですが、本と別売りではありません。このCDがお使いのシステムと互換性がない場合には、当社は責任を負いません。

ビジネス目的で使用しない場合には、イメージの1回の使用には使用料はかかりません。商業目的や、ビジネスを目的で使用する場合には(すべての種類の印刷物への使用、デジタル使用を含みます)ザ・ペピン・プレス/アジャイレ・ラビット・エディションズから、事前の許可を得ることが必要です。

ペピン・プレス/アジャイレ・ラビットのCD-ROMは高品質で、ほとんどのアプリケーションに十分なサイズです。もっと大きなサイズのファイル、あるいはベクトル化したファイルについては、ザ・ペピン・プレス/アジャイレ・ラビット・エディションズあてにご注文ください。

使用許可と使用料については、下記までお問い合わせください。
Eメール:mail@pepinpress.com
ファクス: +31 20 4201152

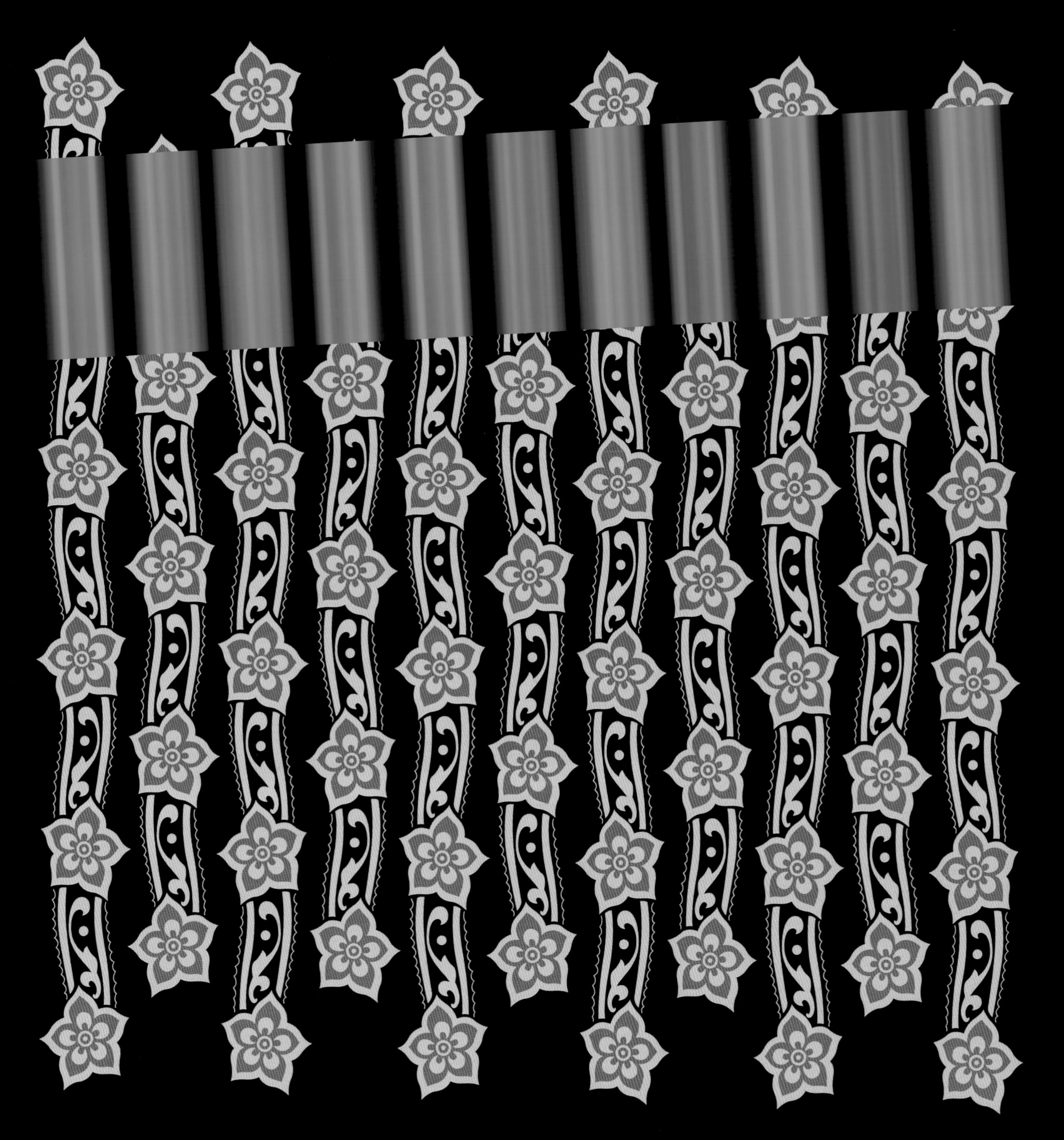

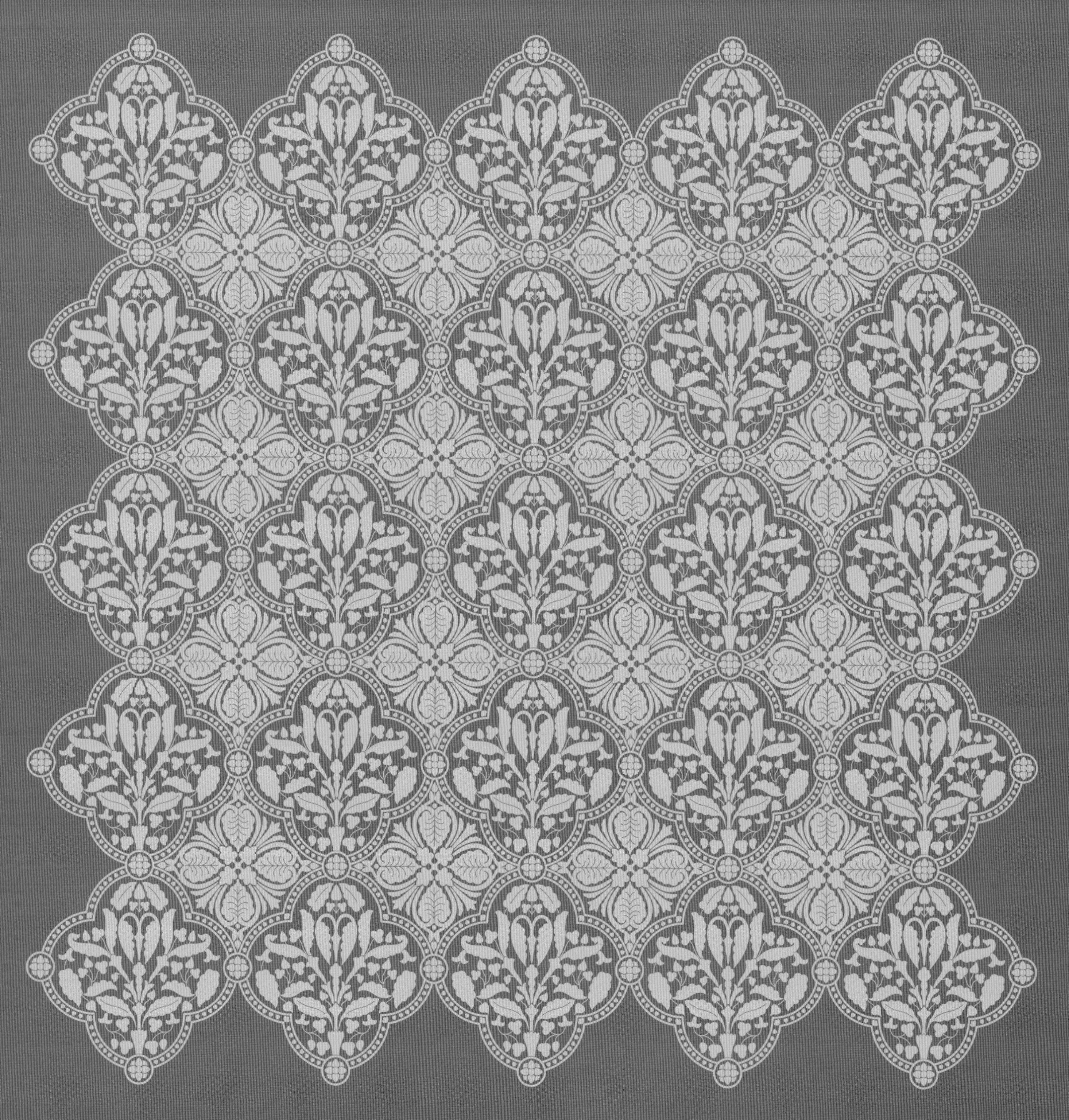

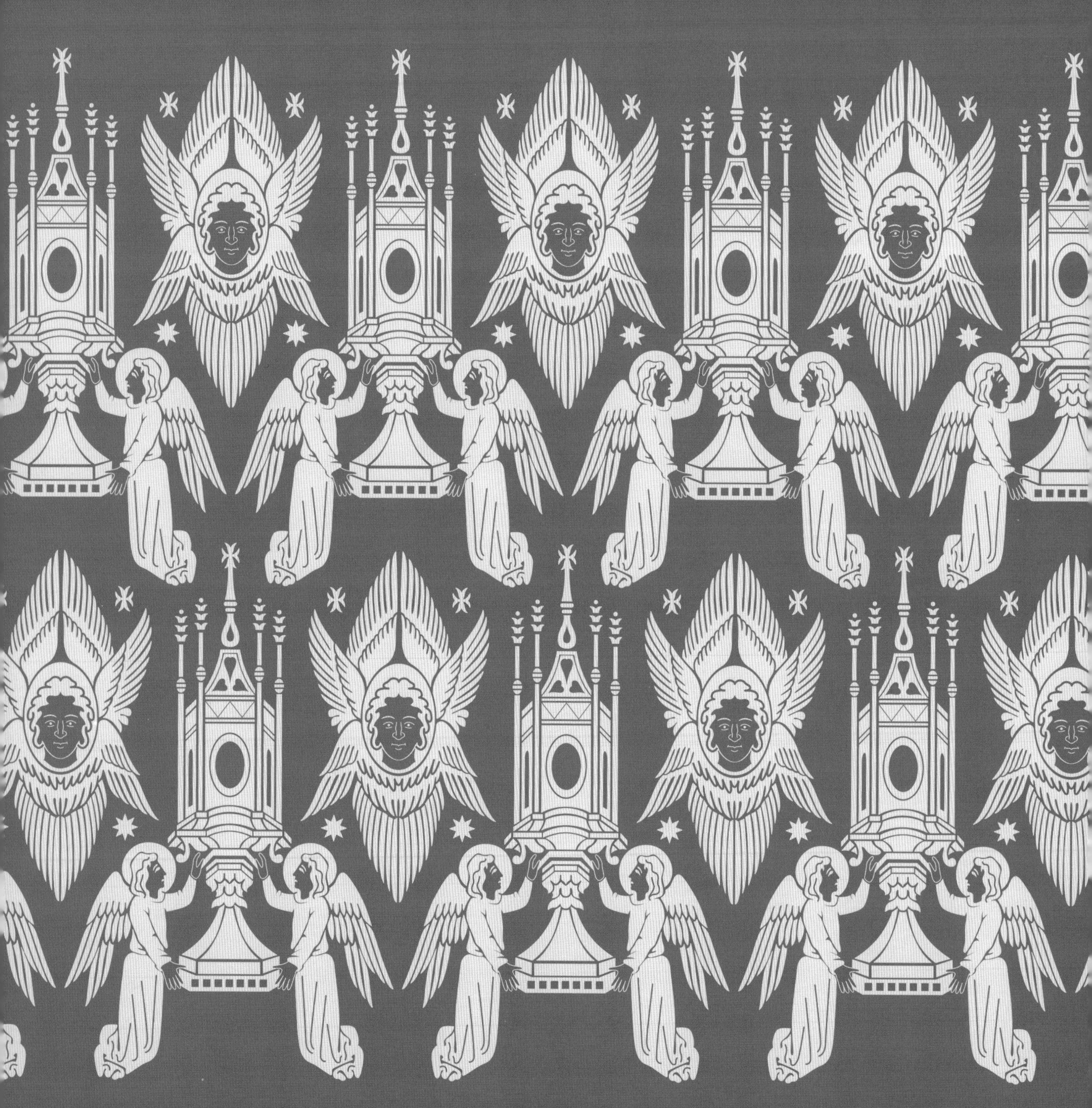

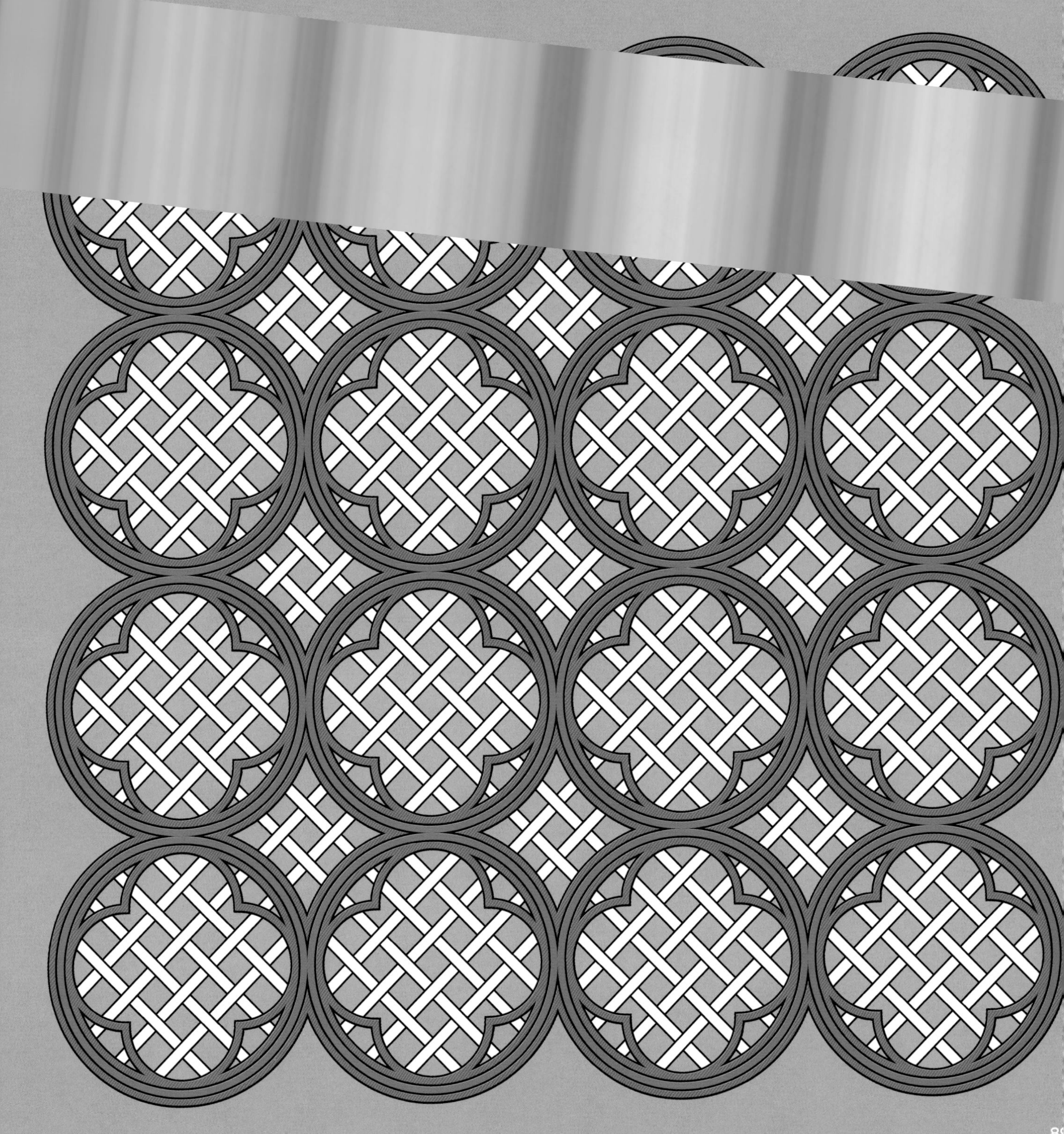

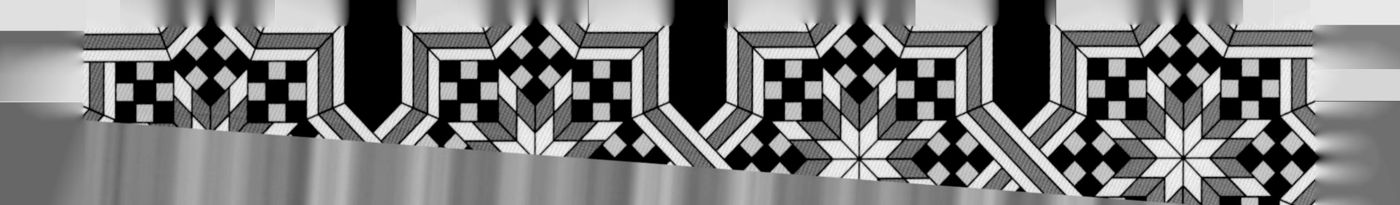

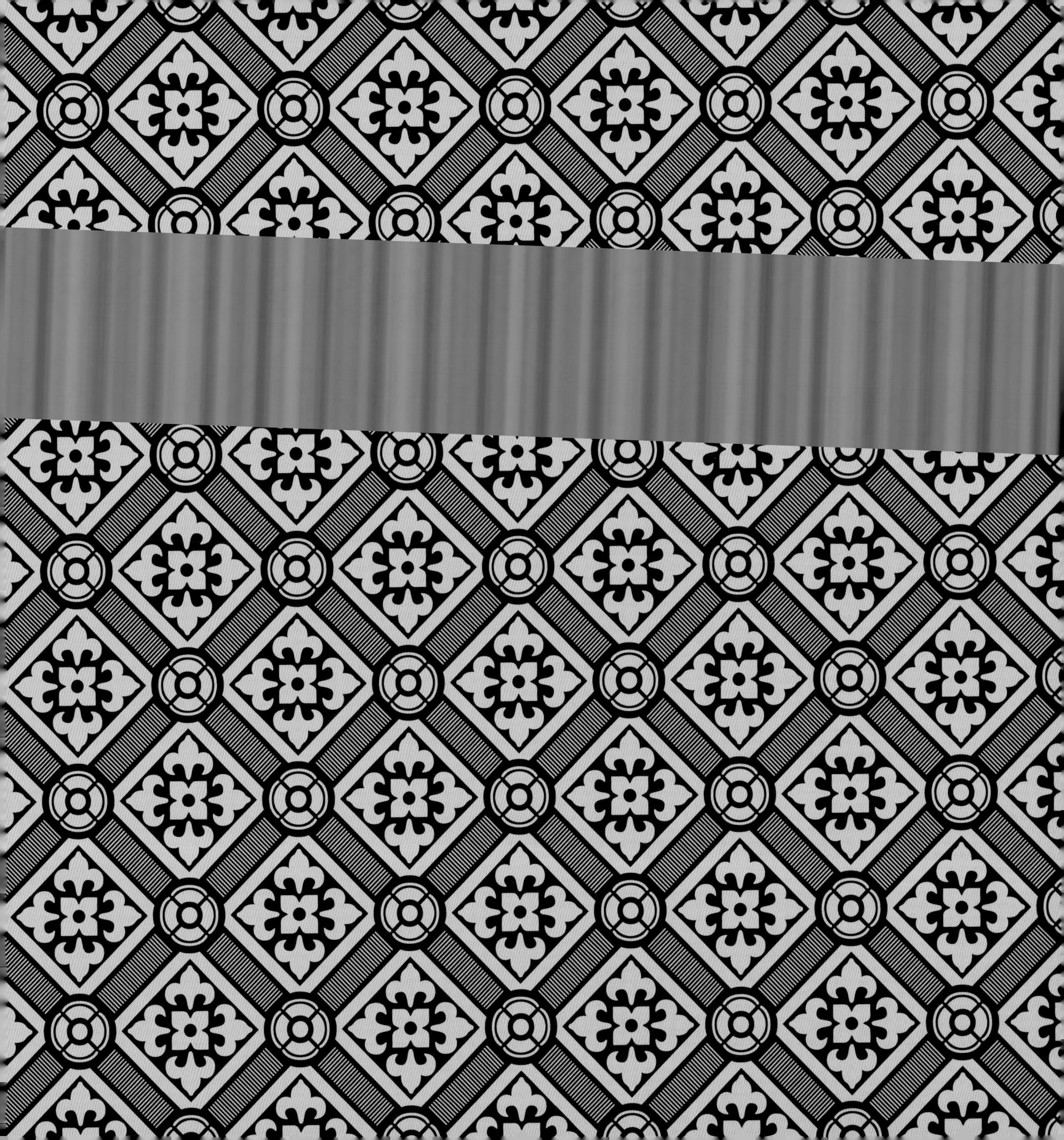

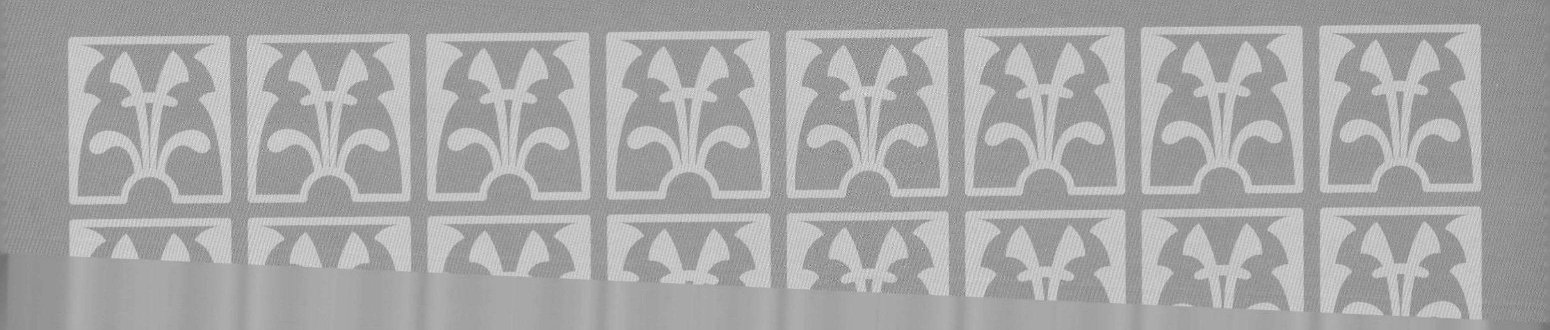

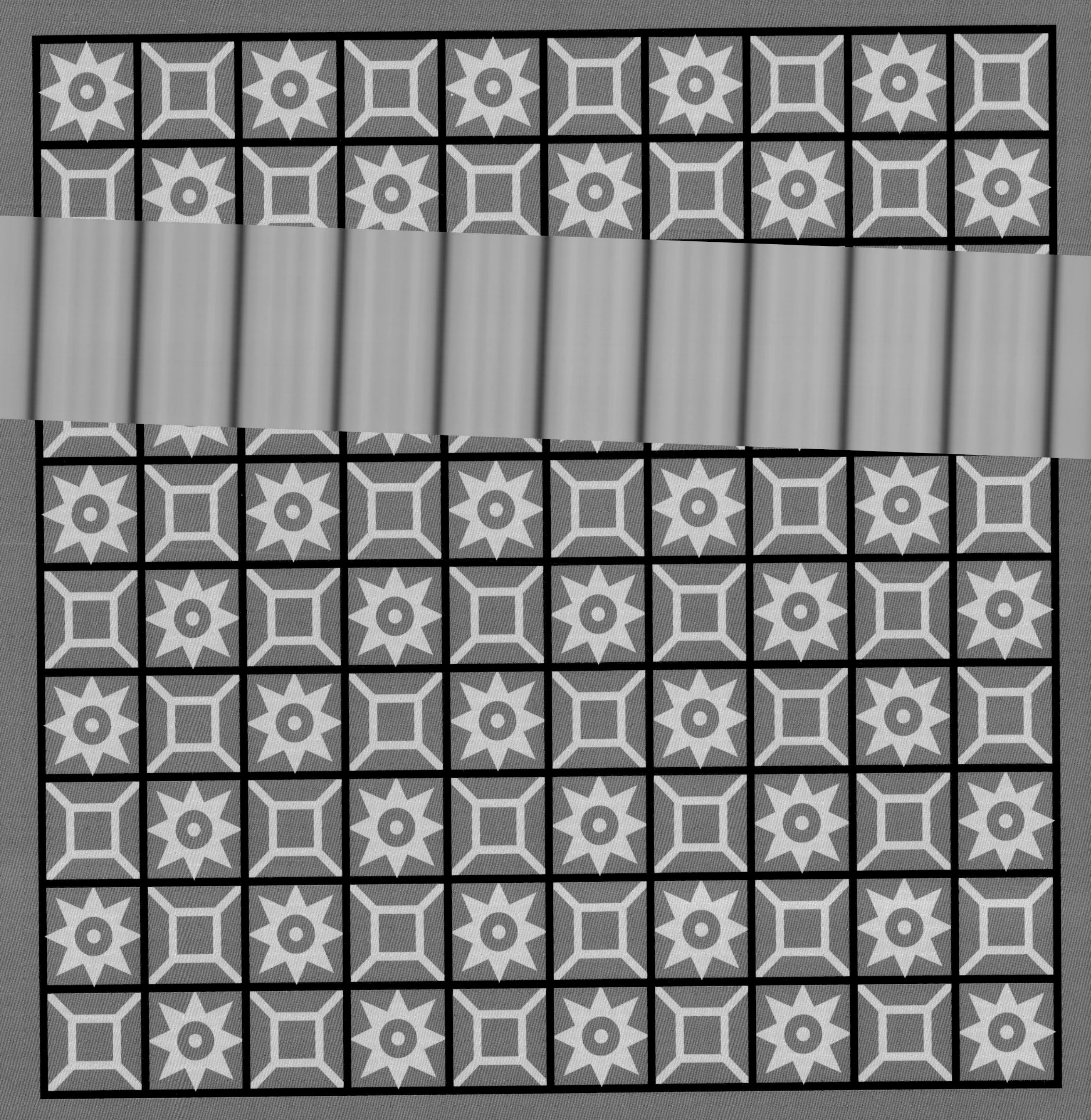

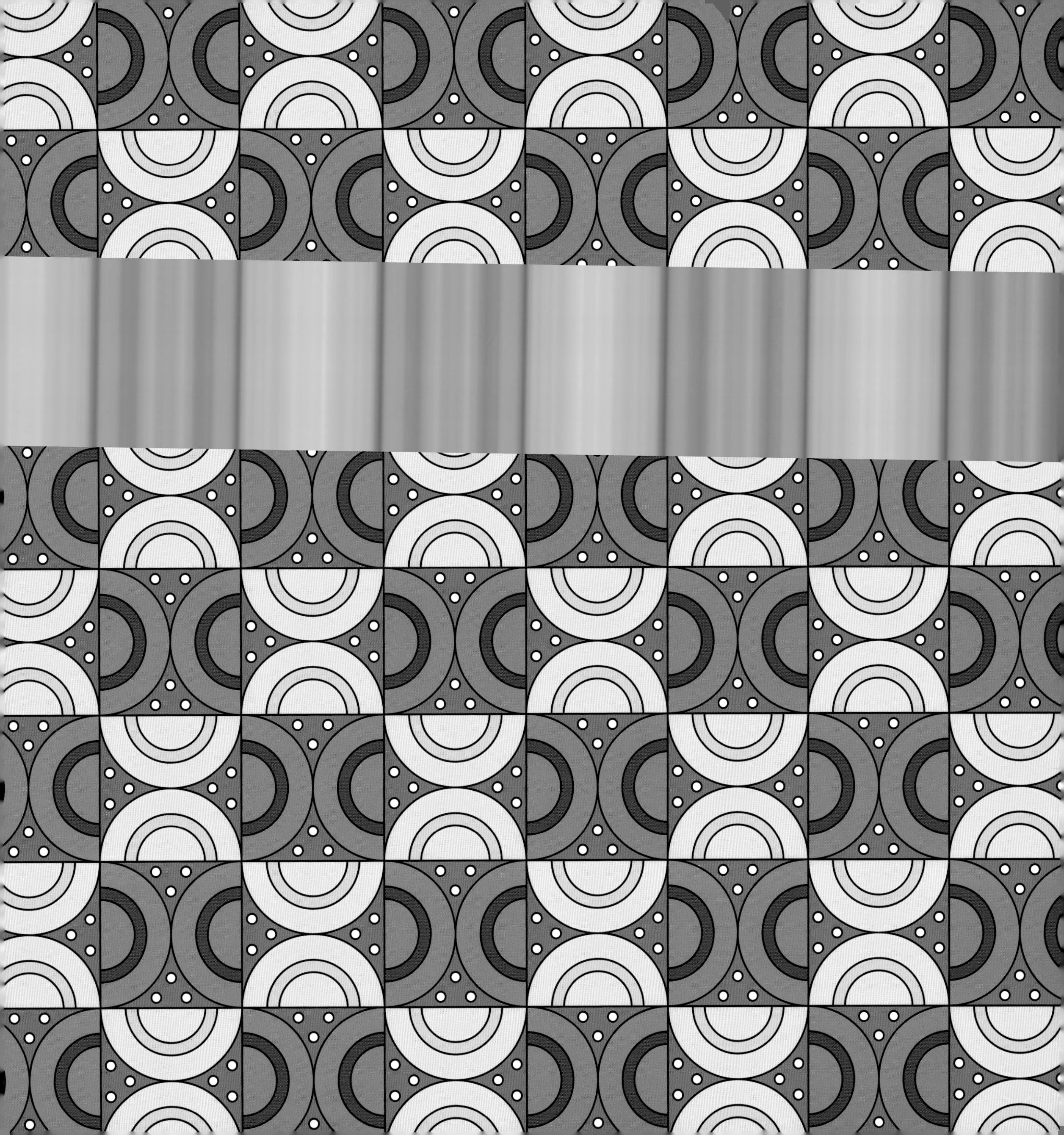

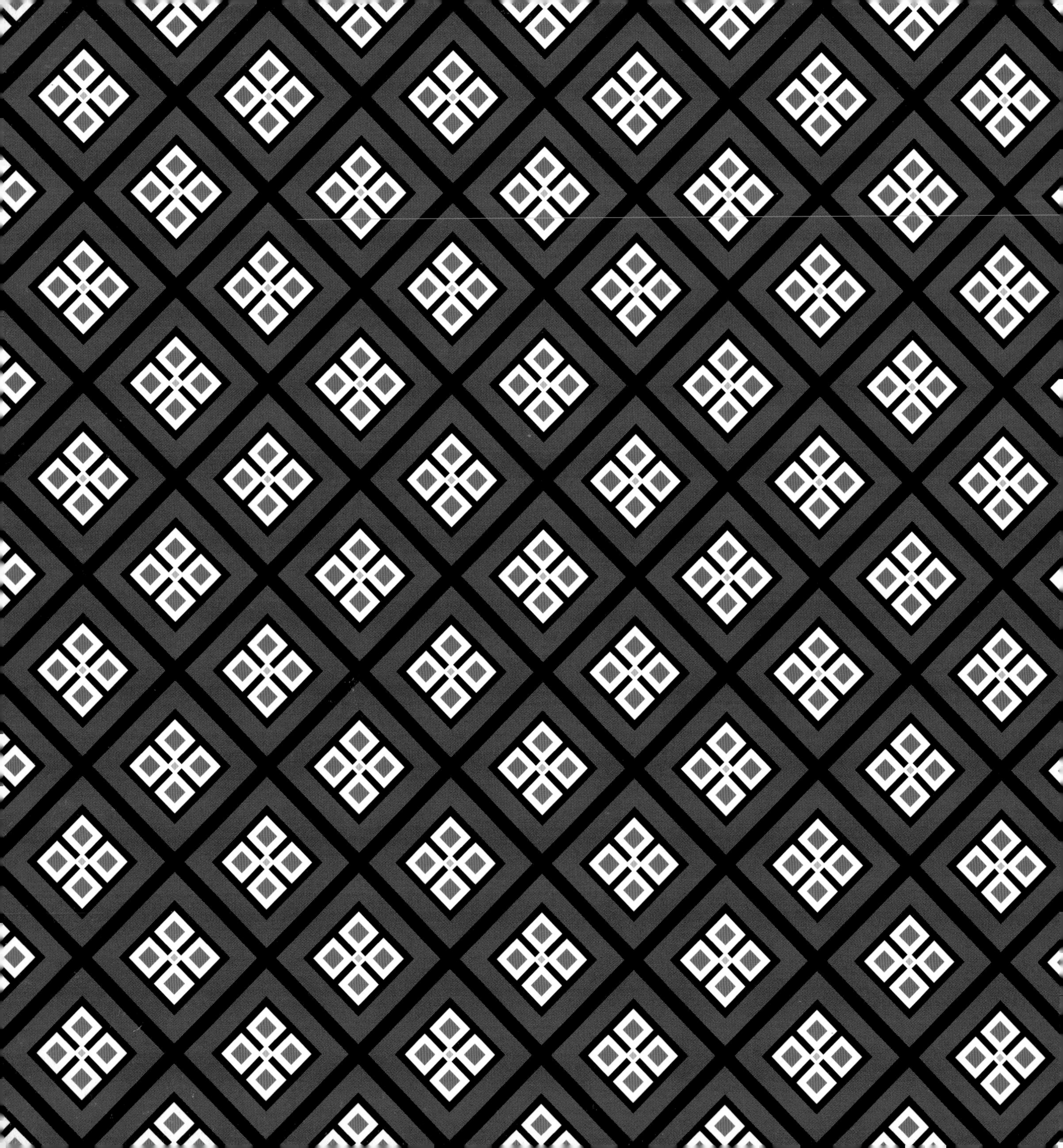